INSIDE

THE

INSURANCE
INDUSTRY

Kevin L. Glaser

CPCU, CIC, SCLA, ARM, AAI, AIC, ARM-P, AIS

Revised © 2010 Kevin L. Glaser. All rights reserved.

ISBN 978-0-557-30029-7

Limit of Liability/Disclaimer of Warranty:

The author and the publisher make no representations or warranties with respect to the accuracy or completeness of the contents of this work and specifically disclaim all warranties, including without limitation warranties of fitness for a particular purpose. No warranty may be created or extended by sales or promotional materials. The advice and strategies contained herein may not be suitable for every situation.

This publication is designed to provide accurate and authoritative information in regard to the subject matter covered. It is sold with the understanding that neither the author nor the publisher is engaged in rendering legal, accounting, insurance advice, or other professional services or advice. If legal advice or other expert assistance is required, the services of a competent professional person should be sought.

Neither the publisher nor the author shall be liable for damages arising here from. The fact that an organization or other specific information is referred to in this work as a citation and/or a potential source of further information does not mean that the author or the publisher endorses the information the organization may provide or recommendations it may make. Further, readers should be aware that information contained in the contents of this publication continually changes, and may have changed between when this work was written and when it is read.

No part of this publication may be reproduced, stored in a retrieval system, or transmitted in any form or by any means, electronic, mechanical, photocopying, recording, scanning, or otherwise, except as permitted under section 107 or 108 of the 1976 United States copyright act, without the prior written permission of the author and publisher. Requests to the author for permission should be addressed to Kevin Glaser, 158 E. Wisconsin Ave., Oconomowoc, WI, 53066.

Table of Contents

Acknowledgements

There are a great many people who deserve my thanks and appreciation for providing guidance and assistance to me throughout my professional career. However, there are none more deserving of my endearing gratitude than my immediate family.

Some twenty years ago my wife, my 2-year old son and myself moved several hundred miles from our hometown to Wisconsin. We left behind friends and family for a new adventure and had no one to rely upon but ourselves. First and foremost, I wish to thank my wonderful wife, Patty, for all of the support she has given to me throughout our 26 years of marriage. She willingly moved to a new home in a far-away state, encouraged me to start an insurance and risk management consulting business from scratch, and has been the rock upon whom I have leaned for so many years. She continues to be the person I rely upon more than anyone else, and I am blessed to have her in my life.

I am also grateful to my oldest son, Nick, for the many special talents that he shares with me and the rest of our family. Nick is a young professional starting his insurance career and learning as much as he can about this industry. Nick provided the impetus for me to publish **Inside the Insurance Industry** and he provided back-end support via proof-reading and formatting this publication. Without him, this book would never have been published.

Many thanks to my college sophomore son, Greg, for providing several insights during his tenure at my consulting business over the summer. Greg has the ability to look at things many different ways and provided me with valuable input while working at Risk & Insurance

Services Consulting, LLC (RISC). He also became quite adept at performing general building repairs during his time spent at **RISC** – including, but not limited to, plumbing-related work.

Becky, my high school junior, also deserves my thanks and gratitude due to the many talents that she possesses and shares with me and our family. She is a talented singer, musician, actress, basketball and softball player, and she manages to achieve outstanding grades while staying so actively involved in school. Her various involvements allow me to step outside of the insurance and risk management world and helps to remind me of the importance of staying well-rounded in life.

Lastly, I am thankful to my 8th grade daughter, Briana, for her quick wit, natural intelligence, piano skills, and "fun to be with" personality. She was recently presented with a respected community-wide award for her many good works throughout the Oconomowoc area. Briana's extra-curricular activities make me proud that she is thinking of so many others at her young age.

Prologue

In my twenty-five plus years in the insurance industry, I have witnessed many changes. One thing that has not changed is the confusion surrounding insurance products that are sold to customers. People have a difficult time understanding what they are buying (or what is being "sold" to them). This publication will help you to understand the inside workings of insurance companies and will allow you to make more educated insurance purchasing decisions.

1

Insurance Company Operating Structure

Insurance companies are typically "*mutual*" or "*stock*" companies. A mutual company is owned by its policyholders. A stock company is owned by its stockholders. There are pros and cons to each type of company charter. The **main advantage** of a *mutual* company from a consumer's perspective is the possibility of receiving a "refund" in the way of a policy dividend if the insurance company's profit-making results are better than anticipated. In other words, if the company makes money based upon the rate (price) it charges, after paying claims and other expenses, it can refund a portion of these profits to its policyholders. Such refunds may take the form of rate *reductions* or *maintaining current insurance product pricing* – rather than taking a rate increase.

The **main advantage** of a *stock* company is that they tend to be priced very competitively up front because they want to bring money in the door to try to make a profit. Profits that are realized are typically paid out to stockholders. Stock companies have an additional advantage in the fact that they can sell more stock if they need to raise capital for any multitude of reasons. In the past several years, a significant number of mutual companies converted to stock companies in order to acquire other companies, to expand their product offerings and to grow the geographical territories in which they were conducting business.

Insurance companies operations differ according to the type of product **distribution method** they have chosen. Major insurance product distribution methods include: *independent agency system*; *exclusive agency system*, and *direct writer* structures.

In the *independent agency system*, agents sell the products of many different insurance companies. Basically, these agencies are individually-owned, profit-oriented businesses, much like a local appliance store that sells several different manufacturer brand names. In reality these independent agencies act as "manufacturer's representatives" for insurance companies. Independent insurance agents advertise individually, as part of trade associations (i.e. the Professional Insurance Agents [PIA]) and under the marketing umbrella of insurance carriers they represent. Usually, the insurance agent pays for part of the advertising and the insurance company pays for part of the advertising. This type of arrangement is known as "co-op advertising," which is short for cooperative advertising. An example of this type of arrangement is an insurance agency that represents and sells insurance for CNA or CHUBB.

Exclusive agents (also referred to as "Captive Agents") must place business with one insurance company, but often have the flexibility to run their offices as they see fit. Agents who represent such insurers may be considered "*independent contractors*," by some insurance companies (i.e. ALLSTATE) but as "*employees*" by others (i.e. STATE FARM and LIBERTY MUTUAL). Many exclusive agents are restricted by contract from submitting business to any other company unless the application is first rejected by the agent's captive company.

Marketing of insurance products is typically the responsibility of the insurance company, although exclusive agents can also mount their own marketing campaigns in order to gain name recognition in their communities.

With *direct writers*, insurance is sold by an *employee* of an insurance company and all business must be written exclusively with that insurer. The ownership of policy expirations lies solely with the insurance company. In order to market their insurance products, many direct writing companies use *television* and *print advertising, telephone, web-related* or *mail solicitation* to sell their insurance products to the public. Many times, direct writers will combine several different sales methods to market their products. Examples of direct writer insurance companies include GEICO and USAA.

It is important to understand that the marketing of insurance products has changed over the past several years and that it is constantly evolving. For example, *telephone marketing* was prevalent in the past. However, with the advent of "do not call" lists in several states, other marketing methods have become the focus of all insurance companies. *Internet marketing* has seen exponential growth. Blogs, website enhancements (including the tracking of visitors), twitter postings and more, have become commonplace. Some companies are even testing the sending of targeted cell phone advertisements to potential insurance customers.

Insurance agents, themselves, are also using the internet in a variety of ways in order to generate new leads, and hopefully, new sales.

Important Terminology

Before leaving the area of insurance product distribution, it is important to discuss one frequent area of consumer confusion. Some insurance agents refer to themselves as "**insurance agents**" and others refer to themselves as "**insurance brokers**." What is the difference?

Insurance agents have signed contracts to represent insurance companies and to sell the products offered by these insurance companies. As a result, legally, they have a *dual fiduciary responsibility* to both the insurance companies they represent and to the customers that buy the insurance policies that they sell.

Insurance brokers technically represent their *customers*, not insurance companies. While there remains a **legal** differentiation between insurance agents and insurance brokers, in **practical** terms there is **no difference**. Insurance brokers today have signed contracts in effect with a multitude of insurance companies, just as independent insurance agents do.

In fact, a few years ago, insurance brokers were the focus of the State of New York's Attorney General, Eliot Spitzer, for *"bid-rigging"* – in direct conflict with the broker's legal duty to their customer. The situation in Mr. Spitzer's case involved a large insurance brokerage that controlled *which* insurance companies would provide bids, as well as the *prices* that the insurance companies would provide for the coverages requested. As a result of the Attorney General's investigation, the area of "**contingent commissions**" became a topic of concern.

Contingent commissions are typically paid on an annual basis, predicated upon the results achieved during the prior twelve-month timeline. These commissions are paid to insurance agents and brokers by insurance companies when certain specific criteria are met. These criteria generally include things such as:

- Premium dollar growth

- Percentage of book of business growth

- Loss ratio results (typically less than 50% pure loss ratio)

- Policy retention percentages (usually better than 80%)

- Miscellaneous other factors, such as book of business rollovers; premium growth in specific industries or at specific agency branch locations, etc.

As a result of public backlash, several large insurance agencies and brokers (but not all of them) decided to no longer accept contingent commissions. Today, many of the agencies and brokers that refused to accept contingent commissions are re-evaluating this position. Some feel that as long as they fully disclose their potential to obtain contingent commission income (what they consider to be *"transparency"*), it should be acceptable to once again enter into some type of additional commission agreements with insurance carriers. Currently, some brokers are accepting *"enhanced commissions"* from insurance carriers with the blessing of their customers.

An *important caveat* to purchasers of insurance: the bid-rigging type of situation that was exposed by Eliot Spitzer in the past is **still** going on today. Part of the reason for this is the insurance placement process. Agents and brokers continue to be in control of which insurance companies are involved in the insurance bidding process, as well as presenting the ultimate insurance proposal (coverages and prices) that is delivered to their customers.

Examples of insurance *brokers* include <u>AON</u>, <u>MARSH</u> and <u>A.J. GALLAGHER & CO.</u> Some well-known larger insurance *agencies* include <u>SIAA</u> (Hampton, NH), <u>LOCKTON COMPANIES</u> (Kansas City, MO) and <u>MESIROW FINANCIAL</u> (Chicago, IL).

Please note that the words "agent" and "broker" will be used interchangeably in this book since both terms to refer to the vernacular of a representative that sells for an insurance company.

2

Insurance Company Internal Department Functions

The **major** internal departments in insurance companies are: *Marketing, Claims, Underwriting, Loss Control* and *Policy Services.* Other **support positions** include: *Legal, Actuary, Subrogation, Internal Audit, Product Development, Information Technology* and *Management.* Each of these will be discussed separately.

Marketing

Marketing consists of both an *internal* and an *external* sales force. *Internal* marketing consists of individuals who are insurance company employees, who "sell" to, or support, the company's chosen distribution channel. *External* sales forces are comprised of the independent agency or exclusive agency agents that sell the insurance company's products. These external salespersons are often categorized as "sales" rather than "marketing," but both are involved in the process of influencing the ultimate decision-maker, the consumer, to buy their company's insurance product. Note that the direct writer company's marketing department fulfills **both** internal and external sales functions.

If "independent" agents are used, the insurance company's *marketing representatives* work to convince agents who have contracts with their company that they should be selling their company's products.

Where captive or exclusive agents are used, *internal marketing* provides sales assistance to the individual agent - such as training; acting as a liaison between agents and the company to help when there is a problem; and assisting in writing new insurance policies – referred to as "new accounts."

Internal marketing also keeps others in the insurance company abreast of what competing companies are doing in the marketplace, and may provide assistance in development of new products or making changes to existing products.

External marketing (or "sales force") sells the insurance company's products to the final customer via the individual company's chosen distribution path. As mentioned earlier, these distribution methods include independent agents, captive agents and direct sales. There are pros and cons to each method of insurance sales from a customer's point of view.

Even though independent agents tout the fact that they do not work for any single insurance company, and do, in fact, have a duty to work in the best interests of their customers, they also have a fiduciary (legal) duty to each of the companies that they represent. This sets the stage for possible conflicts of interest.

Agents who sell the products of one company must sell whatever is available to them via that single company -- no matter how good or bad it is. Companies that have chosen this method of distribution typically put much more emphasis on the "sales" process. The people who sell their products are well-trained salespersons who learn how to sell around all types of objections.

Interestingly, many insurance agents are people who were previously sports "stars," or have otherwise been involved in activities that result in name recognition in the communities where they sell insurance. In reality, these insurance agents may be people through whom some mid-life crisis males (or females) have vicariously lived when such sports/public figure was at the top of his or her game. If a person does not have a well-known public profile, the person who wants to get into insurance sales must typically have somewhere between 100 to 1,000 "*leads*" to contact prior to starting their insurance sales career path.

Once hired as an insurance agent and the initial 100 to 1,000 leads have been exhausted, how are additional leads generated? There are a number of methods. They can be *purchased from outside companies* who specialize in this sort of thing. They can come as a result of *advertising*. However, the most popular method is to develop and work off of a list of "*referrals*." Referrals come about when a person or business seeks out an agent based on something positive they have heard about the person, or where one of the agent's existing customers provides the name of a friend or business associate to the agent. In a best-case scenario, the insurance agent's existing customers pave the way for the agent to contact their personal friends or business associates.

While this latter method is the most popular way of making insurance sales, it does not necessarily result in the best situation for the insurance consumer. Many times the power of a referral is so strong that the buyer asks very few important questions, such as those relating to the experience and qualifications of the person selling insurance policies (refer to the section, "*Some questions you should ask a prospective insurance agent*" found later in this book).

Incentives are often used by companies to generate activity (new business production) on the part of their agency sales force. Captive insurance companies appeal to their agents' desire for money and prestige (i.e. publishing their names in company-wide newsletters or making it to the top-tier "President's Club"), as well as continued employment. Independent insurance companies offer exotic trips (cruises, trips to Switzerland and Hong Kong, etc.) and additional commissions (over and above "contingent commissions" discussed earlier and below) for selling *their* products instead of a competitor's product.

The issue of "contingent commissions" has been touched upon earlier. However, it merits further discussion. Remember, contingent commissions are additional commission dollars that are paid to agencies when certain, contractually agreed-upon criteria are met. Examples of when contingent commissions might be paid include:

- "x-amount" of new business production is written with an insurance company;
- "x-percentage" of profitability on the book of business that exists with the insurance company (usually determined by the *loss ratio* performance of the book of business); or
- a combination of these, or other, criteria

These incentives are rarely, if ever, discussed with the insurance consumer. In some ways, contingent commissions are no different than bonuses paid in other types of industries based upon certain criteria stated in the contract between, for instance, a manufacturer and their manufacturer's representative's (similar in many respects to an insurance company and their appointed insurance agent) agreed-upon performance.

However, there is clearly the possibility that an insurance agent is writing your insurance policy with an insurance company just to earn a better bonus for himself or herself - rather than because that is the best company for you to be written with. Make certain that your agent is not placing you with an insurance company to better his/her own self-interest by specifically asking if they are earning additional compensation by selling a particular insurance policy to you.

Claims

An insurance policy is nothing more (or less) than a contract. The contract is a promise by the insurance company to pay if an "event" occurs which is covered under the terms of the contract. The *claims adjusters* are the ones who interpret whether or not a claim that is presented is an "event" that is covered under the policy (contract) purchased.

The *claims department* consists of adjusters who may work strictly *inside*, or who may work strictly *outside* (in the field), or a *combination* of the two. Simply put, adjusters are the people who control the insurance company's checkbook. Theirs is a difficult job because their company may criticize them for paying too much money on a claim, while their policyholders may criticize them for not paying enough!

Know this: claims adjustors have a fair amount of leeway in deciding how much money a policyholder or a claimant will ultimately be paid. The adjusters who excel in their positions are the ones who get claims closed while paying the least amount of money. Additional kudos is earned by keeping customers happy, but many times this is a secondary consideration.

An adjuster may, albeit infrequently, consult with an *underwriter* (refer to the *"underwriting"* section for additional information on this position) for their "intent" of a specific insurance policy coverage provision, since underwriters are many times involved with drafting of specific policy language. However, the ultimate decision whether or not to pay a claim lies with the adjuster. Most insurance companies follow ISO (Insurance Services Office), which promulgates the vast majority of insurance policy coverage language used by insurance companies today. Because of the wide use of specific insurance policy language, many insurance policy provisions are "court tested," and, as a result, case law exists for many coverage disputes. Adjusters use *case law, internal insurance company claims handling guidelines*, and other *reference/resource materials* when adjusting claims.

Adjusters become aware of case law from sources such as insurance company claims management, internal and external attorneys and from claims-focused magazines and periodicals. Reference materials that may be used by adjusters include items such as: FC&S; ISOnet; NCCI materials; IRMI materials; National Underwriter materials; Rough Notes materials; National Alliance For Insurance Education and Research materials; A.M. Best's materials, and a variety of other resources.

While many events are black-and-white concerning whether or not the policy should respond to a given claim, there are many gray areas where a company may elect to deny payment rather than pay a claim – because that decision is monetarily in their best interest. As stated earlier, in these types of situations, claims adjustors might question underwriters – or employees in the policy development department – to ascertain what the "intent" of coverage was when the particular policy language in question was drafted.

Note, however, that if the policy language is not **clearly** stated in the policy, the policyholder typically prevails should the disagreement move to the court system. Courts view the insurance contract as strictly enforceable because the policyholder has no say in the development of the contract (this is known as a "contract of adhesion"). As a result, ambiguities are decided in favor of the insurance consumer. However, the problem becomes how long and how hard does a policyholder want to fight about coverage issues? Often, they give up too soon or forego use of an *attorney, consultant,* or a *public adjuster,* whereas the attorney, consultant or public adjuster may be able to resolve a claim in the policyholder's favor.

An example from my own insurance company experience will drive this point home. One of the companies I worked for (which is no longer writing insurance coverages) offered a coverage called "*voluntary property damage,*" which was often purchased by contractors (landscape gardeners, carpenters, plumbers, electricians, etc.). The intent of the coverage endorsement was to delete an exclusion in the general liability portion of the insurance policy that pertained to property in the policyholder's care, custody or control. For instance, if I am a painter and I go inside of your house to paint a room, the entire room I will be painting is deemed to be in my care, custody or control. If I happen to poke a hole in the wall with my ladder, the hole in the wall is something that will **not** be covered by my insurance policy. The voluntary property damage endorsement was meant to provide coverage for this type of situation.

However, the way my prior employer worded the endorsement, intended coverages were not actually provided by the endorsement in a great number of care, custody or control claims situations. While there was not a huge premium charge for the endorsement, it was sold for many years without technically providing coverage for several claims related to care, custody or control – which was why the endorsement was developed to begin with.

It would have been relatively easy to add additional coverage by clarification of policy language intent, but this was never done. Why not? Due to the small premium charge, it wasn't worth the insurance company's time and effort to correct the problem. It would have taken considerable time for the people from the Information Technology department to re-program the computers, time for people from the Policy Development Department to recommend new wording, time to provide updates and training to the Underwriting and Claims Department advising of the new wording, and so forth. Clearly, this decision was not in the best interest of the policyholder, but it was deemed a good business decision by insurance company management on a purely "cost of change" basis.

Consumers remain confused about the insurance claims process mainly because of the lack of information and the great amount of misinformation that has been spread by friends, relatives, neighbors and others concerning insurance claims. Common types of property claims include: hail, wind, lightning, water and theft. And, while not frequent, fire is still one of the most catastrophic types of property claims that occur.

Other events which may result in significant claims include personal liability, at-fault automobile accidents, on-premises medical injuries, and other types of situations where policyholders are deemed legally liable ("negligent") in some manner. It is interesting to note that, according to recent statistics, in the realm of homeowners claims, property and theft claims account for nearly 80% of all claims payments, while liability claims account for less than 10%.

Please understand that there are *very few* hard and fast rules in the area of claims. There are several reasons for this. First, each claim must *stand on its own merits.* The facts surrounding each claim are all-important. For example, a hail storm occurs. Two next door neighbors turn claims into their respective insurance companies. One day soon after, the neighbors are talking and discover that one of them got a claim check from their insurer for $4,500 to replace his roof and the other received no payment at all. In the course of investigating the facts, it was discovered that the neighbor who received a claim payment had a 25-year old roof, and the other had his roof replaced just last year. There is a logical explanation for this claims handling discrepancy. Old roofs are easily damaged, while new roofs are very resilient against hail. Thus, these claims were handled properly.

Second, there is some *flexibility* from insurance company to insurance company in the area of underwriting. One company may file their automobile insurance program with a rule that "forgives" the policyholder's first automobile physical damage claim if the policyholder has been insured continuously for five or more years. Another company may not have filed this same rule and, instead, surcharges for any at-fault accident which exceeds a stated threshold dollar amount, such as $500.

Third, there are "*gray areas*" in the insurance policy. It is impossible for insurance policies to contemplate every single claim situation that might ever arise. Do you have a hard time believing this? As an expert witness in court for insurance-related cases, I assure you this is true. Courts are constantly addressing insurance policy coverage questions.

Some of the many questions that insurance consumers have concerning claims include:

- Will my policy be cancelled if I turn in a claim?
- Will my insurance rates increase if I make a claim?
- Am I better off paying small claims out of pocket, or should I turn in every claim?
- Are claims under my business insurance policy viewed in the same way that claims are viewed under my personal insurance policies?
- What are my options if coverage for my claim is denied by my insurance company?

For the reasons previously outlined, keep in mind that there may be different outcomes in the way that adjusters will handle two "similar" claims. Nevertheless, below are possible answers to the above questions to provide you with insight into these claims-related questions.

Will my policy be cancelled if I turn in a claim? Maybe - depending on the type of claim, the number of claims you have made in a specific time period, and the underwriting criteria in place at your insurance company.

Will my insurance rates increase if I make a claim? Generally, homeowner policies will not go up. However, automobile policies may - depending on underwriting criteria and who was at-fault.

Am I better off paying small claims out of pocket, or turning in each claim? It may benefit you <u>not</u> to turn in small claims. It does, however, depend upon on the type of claim and the facts involved. For instance, if $520 of personal clothing is stolen out of your car, and if you carry a $500 deductible, it makes little sense to turn in the claim. However, if someone slips and falls in front of your house on an icy sidewalk that you did not shovel for three days and injures themselves, you <u>should</u> turn in the claim - even if they say they will not hold you liable. This type of claim may turn ugly and it is important to provide your insurance company with information concerning the situation as soon as possible so they can investigate, and hire defense counsel if the need arises.

Are claims under my business insurance policy viewed the same way as claims under my personal insurance policies? No, most business policies are underwritten on a "loss ratio" basis. This means that company underwriters weigh the amount of premiums "paid in" against the amounts of claims dollars "paid out." While different companies apply different profitability criteria, most insurance companies are content with a pure loss ratio of 50% or less. However, the higher the loss ratio, the more likely that a higher renewal price increase will be applied.

Conversely, under homeowners and automobile policies, insurance companies typically take a long, hard look at the frequency of losses incurred. Since homeowners premiums are generally less than $1,000 annually, insurance companies cannot afford to pay out many claims and hope to remain profitable. While automobile insurance rates are somewhat higher, payments for liability and medical claims can involve significant payments. Again, insurance companies cannot pay many high dollar automobile claims for one policyholder and remain profitable. What about a policyholder who has several very small claims? Underwriters apply the following rule: *frequency breeds severity*. In other words, if a policyholder has a history of small claims, a big claim is almost certain to follow at some point in the future.

What are my options if coverage for my claim is denied by my insurance company? A good first step is to discuss the situation with your insurance claims adjustor. Make certain they understand the facts clearly. If they have denied your claim they should cite the specific policy language upon which they rely. If you continue to feel the insurance company has wrongly denied your claim, you should next discuss your claim with your insurance agent. Your agent has a legal, fiduciary responsibility to act in your best interest. Keep in mind, however, they also have a fiduciary obligation to the insurance companies they represent. At times, this can result in their refusal to get involved with claims since agents may feel that adjusters are in the best position to interpret claims.

After discussing your situation with your insurance adjustor and your insurance agent to no avail, you may next wish to discuss your claim denial with a public adjustor, an insurance consultant or an attorney. Also, you may wish to involve the Commissioner of Insurance in your applicable state where coverages apply (typically your "state of domicile") by filing a complaint and asking that they review the circumstances of your claim denial.

Yes, it is possible that your insurance company made a mistake, or that your claim may involve a gray area under the insurance policy where the insurance company has taken the position that benefits them rather than you. However, it has been my experience that the vast majority of insurance claims are handled efficiently and correctly by insurance company adjustors. Therefore, if your insurance claim has been denied, it is quite possible that there truly is no coverage for your claim under your insurance policy.

Keep in mind that payment of claims is the reason insurance companies are in business. However, they must follow their policy (contract) wording during the claims adjustment process. If they pay claims that are not covered under the insurance policy then many other facets of the insurance coverage process is affected, such as:

- Policy rates will go up since actuaries did not contemplate payment for uncovered claims

- Courts may broaden the insurance company's liability for other claims which were never intended to be covered. This can result from a plaintiff's attorney asking the insurance company if they ever intentionally paid claims which were not covered by their insurance contract.

- Claims adjusters, underwriters and the marketing department may become confused concerning coverages provided under insurance policies sold to the public.

Underwriting

Underwriting is the analysis of characteristics of a risk to decide if the risk is *acceptable*, *unacceptable*, or *acceptable if certain requested conditions (changes) are met*. The underwriter reviews applications that are submitted and decides if the characteristics presented meet company guidelines that are in place for that particular class of business (such as homeowners, auto or businessowners policies).

By its very nature, underwriting is discriminatory. Underwriters apply a set of criteria and, many times, are also allowed personal leeway (known as "underwriting judgment") when making decisions on specific accounts.

The underwriter typically has the power to make **"exceptions"** to the company's guidelines and issue a policy based on a submission - even though that submission does not technically qualify. If an exception is made, it is typically documented, and is frequently reviewed by management.

Underwriters also possess **pricing** authority. This is true in both personal lines and commercial lines, though much more evident on large commercial accounts. The most frequent pricing structure used in personal lines (auto and homeowner policies) is application of *"preferred credits,"* or use of a *"tiered"* approach. Whichever method of pricing is used, the idea is that the best risks (those which the company underwriter feels will have no future claims) get the best pricing. This is not always the case, however, as favors are frequently done on the underwriting level based on things such as an underwriter's relationship with an agent.

One of the craziest things about the underwriting process is the archaic *rating methodology* that is used to price commercial lines (business insurance) policies. There is no good (quick and easy-to-use) rating system that is widely available in the insurance industry.

Some insurance companies have developed proprietary rating systems and do provide their field underwriters with the capability to price insurance products outside of the office. However, once the insurance products are quoted in the field, arcane rating systems are used back at the home office in order to get insurance policies issued.

A tremendous amount of effort and time is required to rate coverages that the insurance company provides. All the customer and agent want is a bottom line price. They don't care how difficult it is to massage the insurance company's computer software to come up with a price. Much of the problem has to do with the history of commercial lines rate-making and the fact that "it has always been done this way." What is needed is a major overhaul of the commercial lines products rating methodologies in order to simplify the way that accounts are priced. The result will be a welcome reduction in the amount of time it takes to issue a commercial insurance policy, as well as a better understanding by consumers of how prices are determined (better "transparency").

Policy Services

Policy Services provides the internal assistance necessary for the insurance company to get their policies issued. This includes rating entry, secretarial-related work, and other jobs that move a policy through the organization and out their doors.

Many insurance companies also include some type of "quality control" as part of their Policy Services Department. Quality control entails the review of issued policies to ascertain whether they contain the policy forms, endorsements, exclusions and other items that match the insurance coverage requested by the consumer.

Amazingly enough, some insurance companies have done away with the quality control function. For example, during a recent deposition I discovered that a large, national insurance company relies completely upon their insurance agents to review issued policies for accuracy. The attorney for the insurance carrier stated that the insurance company feels it is the responsibility of their insurance agent representatives to review policies as part of the services the agency provides to earn the commissions paid by the insurance company. I find this stance utterly amazing. This position is similar to a manufacturer putting out a product and expecting their manufacturer's representative to perform a quality control review of their product. Common sense dictates that the party that has the most knowledge about the product being produced should implement quality control procedures.

Audit Department

The main purpose of the *Audit Department* is to find out if there have been changes in a commercial policy since the last anniversary date. Many commercial insurance policies are issued on an "auditable" basis. This means that the initial insurance premium is based upon an "estimate" – a best-guess as to what the business exposure will be at the end of the policy term. Auditable insurance policies include: General Liability; Worker's Compensation; Business Automobile, and certain other policies, such as Commercial Inland Marine and some Non-Standard insurance policies. Auditable policies are rated based upon estimated "exposures." For General Liability, rating may be based upon things such as square footage (area), gross sales receipts, units, payroll, admissions, or "A-Rates," where underwriting judgment is used to determine a rate to charge for the exposure. For Worker's Compensation, rates are based upon worker job duties (classifications) and payrolls assigned to each classification on the current policy.

Here is an **example** of an auditable policy situation: Acme Widgets has an insurance policy that is effective January 1, 2009, and expires on January 1, 2010. Acme plans sales of $1,000,000 during the 2009 policy year. Therefore, the insurance policy is issued using a specific rate (i.e. 1.57 per $1,000 of sales), which is chosen by the underwriter. This rate is then applied to the estimated sales value. The policy is issued with a General Liability premium of $1,570, which reflects the 1.57 rate x 1,000 exposure units ($1,000,000 dollars of sales). The policy is audited six months after the end of the policy term (June

30, 2010) and it is discovered that Acme actually sold $2,000,000 of widgets during the policy period.

In this case, an additional premium is developed taking the 1.57 specific rate times 1,000 additional sales exposure units (representing the additional $1,000,000 of sales that took place during 2009). Another $1,570 of premium is owed to the insurance company as a result of the **actual** sales that took place at Acme Widgets. This is fair to all parties because additional sales made represent additional exposure to the insurance company and they are entitled for additional premium to offset the additional risks present. Alternately, if only $500,000 in sales were generated by Acme during 2009, they would be entitled to a credit of $785 for the reduced exposure basis. If a credit is due to the policyholder, a check is issued by the insurance company and sent to the policyholder.

Note that there are some insurance policies that are issued on a "non-auditable" basis. Generally, this is a positive situation for the insurance customer because it allows businesses to better budget their annual insurance costs, and it can result in cost-savings for businesses that are growing. However, for those businesses with declining sales, an auditable policy is still best since they will get money refunded when an audit takes place after the policy period ends.

Loss Control

Loss Control (also known as "*Loss Control Engineering*" or "*Safety Engineering*") is a service offered by insurance companies to clients who meet certain criteria. These include: class of business (a manufacturing business certainly warrants loss control while a small ice cream store generally does not); premiums generated by the account (many insurance companies do not feel it is cost effective to offer these types of services to an account that generates less than $25,000, or so, of annual insurance premium); and on a case-by-case basis (usually as a result of customer or agent request).

Loss control is a valuable service if the individual performing the inspection is well-trained and experienced in looking at the particular type of business you own. Where this potential benefit fails is when the loss control inspector is not knowledgeable, or where he/she does not follow through on specific key recommendations generated during their personal inspection of your business.

Loss control can work miracles in bringing down both **frequency** and **severity** of worker's compensation injuries. Loss control engineers can help implement safety programs and works with human resources, as well as supervisors and foremen, to ensure the success of safety programs. They also address things such as potential products liability claims and whether or not the business is complying with current work-related laws and regulations (i.e. OSHA). However, the number one thing that loss control engineers can do is to get owners or top-level managers involved in key loss control issues. If top management is not 100% behind recommended changes, necessary loss control changes – and resulting business improvements – will simply not occur.

For effective loss control, the insurance company representative should visit the business a minimum of twice per year. Four times to twelve times per year may be necessary, initially, depending on the type of business, the focus of the loss control initiatives (i.e. Worker's Compensation vs. premises liability related) and/or the severity of problems that are discovered. More than likely, the insurance company will not offer this frequency of visits, so it is up to the customer to demand it.

Alternative sources of information are available if your business does not meet the minimum qualifications for insurance company loss control services. These include hiring private loss control engineering firms, requesting an OSHA inspection, or using other state or local government agencies.

A business can request a free OSHA inspection to see if they are in compliance with federal laws. The OSHA inspector will point out areas of non-compliance (if any) and will not levy a fine for any deficient areas discovered during this process.

Other resources may be available, depending on the state where your business is located. For example, in the state of Wisconsin, a Worker's Compensation classification code audit can be provided by an entity known as the Workers Compensation Rating Bureau (WCRB). In the course of their inspection they will also point out safety concerns that they might observe.

3

Other Insurance Company Support Positions

Other positions that support the infrastructure of insurance companies include: *Legal, Actuary, Subrogation, Internal Audit, Product Development, Information Technology* and *Management.*

Legal

The *Legal department* supports the claims department. It ultimately decides which claims should be fought (company position defended), which "outside" attorneys (independent, stand-alone law firms that represent insurance companies and their insureds) will be used in litigation support matters, and at what point a settlement should be considered. In my experience, most "internal" attorneys do not possess the same legal expertise as those attorneys who practice law as a part of a law firm. Thus, "outside" attorneys usually represent the concerns of the insurance company in court.

Company attorneys may also provide support to human resources and other internal departments concerning setting of guidelines and policies, as well as providing guidance on internal claims and suits – such as worker's compensation claims and employment-related practices suits for things such as age discrimination. An ancillary reason that outside attorneys are used by insurance companies is to avoid possible conflict of interest claims by their insureds. If an insurance company uses its own attorneys to represent its insureds, it may be accused of acting in its own best interest – i.e. by trying to pay as little as possible for a claim, regardless of the merits.

An example of this would be a situation where an insurance company's insured was sued as the result of negligent operation of a motor vehicle. If the injuries are substantial and the policy liability limits are low, the insurance company may not even want to spend money on defense of their insured. However, this exposes the policyholder's personal assets. Courts have decided that the duty to defend is as important, if not more important than, the duty to pay for damages.

Another reason outside law firms are used is because of the wide variety of expertise offered by external law firms. It is difficult for internal lawyers to be experts in all areas of law, thus, if expertise is required in special areas such as products liability, product recall, pollution, etc., external attorneys are sought out that possess this specific expertise. Also, external attorneys have more experience in preparing for and presenting the insurance company's position before a judge should the case move to trial.

Actuary

"Kill the actuaries" is the battle-cry of many underwriters and marketing representatives. The purpose of those in the *actuarial department* is to statistically analyze the rate structure of insurance policies by line of business (i.e. commercial property, commercial general liability, commercial automobile, homeowners and personal automobile) to decide whether a rate increase or decrease is needed, and if so, by how much.

Ratemaking is often a matter of massaging the numbers to say what you want them to say. For **example**, actuarial data for the state of Wisconsin may call for an overall increase of 10% on homeowners policies (referred to as "book of business") based upon statistics gathered by the actuarial department. This includes reviewing total premiums (income) received, subtracting expenses such as claims paid and outstanding liabilities (known as "incurred but not reported," or "IBNR" within the industry), and subtracting company expenses – including items such as payroll, benefits, and overhead and profit.

This 10% rate increase recommended by actuarial is then reviewed by marketing and/or underwriting (depending on where the responsibility for this task falls). Joint discussions are then held between these departments, and senior management, to determine the ultimate policy price increase – or decrease – that will be taken. Discussions include things such as statutory rate adequacy, marketing competitiveness, future income and expenses projections (including regulatory impact, time value of money, etc.).

Rate discussions are always a balancing act. The insurance company must charge enough money to stay soluble but cannot charge too much compared to its competition. If pricing gets too far above competitor pricing, the insurance company is likely not only to shut down new business income, but may also lose existing business on the books. The result is that profitability will suffer. An additional factor that insurance companies keep in mind is that their "best" customers will leave (policyholders with good credit ratings, good driving records and claims-free) if prices are raised too much. The customers that are left will be less profitable because of some undesirable underwriting characteristic – and the fact that this may make them viewed as "unacceptable" to another insurance company. This result may further deteriorate the insurance company's bottom-line.

My experience is that a great deal of emphasis is placed upon marketing competitiveness during actuarial discussions. The marketing department often plays a lead role in discussions and is typically successful in convincing senior management that, although actuarial data calls for a 10% statewide increase, a lower percentage of increase should be implemented due to marketplace competitiveness.

Understand that the above example is quite simplified. In actuality, much "fine-tuning" takes place during the ratemaking process. For instance, rates in one territory with poor experience may be supported by another territory with good experience.

This means that, rather than taking a 10% statewide homeowners rate increase, insurance companies' segment rate information using a multitude of factors. Some of these include: age of home; value of home; geographical territory; liability values; protection class and much more. Ultimately, the insurance company's homeowner rates may decrease for homes located in Milwaukee, Wisconsin, but will be offset by taking a 20% increase for those located in Superior, Wisconsin. Therefore, the desired net effect of a 10% overall increase is achieved.

Once new rates are agreed upon, the company files its rates with the department of insurance in the state(s) where the new rates will be in effect. Where a *file-and-use* law is in effect, the insurance company must submit its new rates before they become effective. Actual approval is **not** required before the rates are used. However, the department of insurance can disapprove the rates if they find them in violation of any statutes. To play it safe, a company often waits until the department of insurance has reviewed and approved the rates just to make sure that their company will not need to recall their rates.

If a *prior-approval* law is in effect, all rates must be filed with the state's Department of Insurance (Insurance Commissioner's office) prior to use and must be **formally** approved or disapproved before implemented.

It cannot be over-emphasized that the setting of rates presents many dichotomies, such as, regardless of what the mathematical models may say, the company must compete in the "real world" against other companies trying to sell similar products. If actuary suggests a rate increase of 20% and this puts the insurance company's pricing structure at a total of 15% over marketplace competitors, very little additional new business is likely to be written. On the other hand, by completely ignoring actuary's findings, the company is jeopardizing its surplus (the funds available for paying claims).

Subrogation

Subrogation Department personnel are known as the "bad boys" of the insurance company. They typically work as a part of the claims department and chase down individuals or companies that owe money to the insurance company. If, for instance, an automobile accident occurs where someone other than the policyholder is clearly at fault in damaging the insurance company policyholder's car, or injuring the car's occupants, the policyholder's company may *directly* pay the policyholder for the damage, or provide medical payments.

However, the insurance company will then try to collect what it has paid from the party responsible for the accident. If that person does not have insurance, they will personally owe the amount of damages for the repair of the policyholder's banged-up vehicle (as well as medical payments, etc.) and must ultimately pay any outstanding legal judgment on an out-of-pocket basis. Payment plans, including garnishment of wages, may be set up for repayment of what is owed.

More and more insurance companies are turning their attention to subrogation. Why is this? Because of the potential to recoup dollars paid out to policyholders. Some subrogation efforts amount to thousands or even hundreds of thousands of dollars. However, even small dollar amounts can add up to significant dollar amounts for insurance companies.

In addition, insurance companies are becoming more aggressive pursuing certain specific types of subrogation. For instance, companies are recognizing the potential that Worker's Compensation subrogation holds. Insurance companies must pay Work Comp claims according to state statutes which generally demand payment on a "no fault" basis. In other words, if an employee is injured due to a work-related occurrence, insurance companies must make payment to the employee for the injury that incurred. However, it is possible that the injury was the result of the negligence of a third party (unrelated to the employer). In this situation, the insurance company is entitled to demand payment from the at-fault party. If the negligent party does not agree to make payment based upon the demand letter, the insurance company that made payment is legally entitled to bring a lawsuit against the negligent party for what is owed to the insurance company.

Many times, outside collection agencies or attorneys are used for subrogation purposes. Understand that these people can play hardball! In some of these types of outsourced subrogation situations the subrogation firms are paid based upon a percentage of the total dollar recovery amount. As a result, they are aggressive not only in their attempts to receive payment, but also related to the dollar amount sought.

Internal Audit

The *Internal Audit* department reviews internal insurance company underwriting and claims (and other) department activities to make sure various departments within the insurance company are acting within company guidelines. Many times management requests that a certain underwriting line of business, or a particular type of claim adjuster file (i.e. liability adjuster), be reviewed to see if there are possible areas of improvement. Another reason for internal review of underwriting and claims files is to discover whether any wrongdoing (i.e. fraud) has occurred. Auditors look for both isolated situations as well as patterns of negative activities that have occurred. Auditors review files, note observations and make recommendations for change in the hopes of seeing improvements in the near future.

Internal audit also monitors things such as possible vendor (or agent, etc.) kickbacks to employees, expense report accuracy and they ascertain whether employees are doing their jobs honestly. I have known of situations where claims adjusters have invented a "dummy" corporation and began making claims payments to their dummy corporation for building repairs – while in reality "pocketing" all of the money. I have also seen agents take money from clients but keep the money and pay claims a client might experience out of their own private accounts. Here, insurance policies were never actually issued and the company was unaware that the client ever purchased insurance. Never heard of such a thing? Insurance companies rarely, if ever, report this type of fraud since it gives them very bad press and makes their other policyholders nervous.

Product Development

Insurance companies are a strange lot. They tout their "differences" and reasons why they are better than their competitors. However, at times, companies sell very similar products at similar prices. **Examples** include homeowners, automobile and businessowner package policies. One of the reasons for this is that companies often start out by using the same rates and coverage language as their basis of coverage - items which are provided by the Insurance Services Office (ISO) or the American Association of Insurance Services (AAIS). Since the insurance policy is a contract, insurers are comfortable using contract language that has been "court tested." While prior lawsuits provide valuable case law for insurance carriers, it also ties their hands when it comes to offering innovative products in the marketplace. The result is that many insurance companies sell nearly identical "black boxes."

While customers might want a "black-and-white box," the company says all it can offer is a "black box" - take it or leave it. Many times, the customer is either left unsatisfied, or continues to look for alternate ways to get what he/she wants from an insurance coverage standpoint.

Most companies keep pretty close tabs on what its competitors are up to. If a new product is introduced by the competition, other companies typically wait for six months or so to see how well the product has been received in the marketplace. If the new product has provided decent revenues, while incurring limited claims payments, other companies in essence "copy" the new product that the trend-setting company has introduced.

Everyone at insurance companies keep their eyes and ears open concerning their competition, but typically it is the marketing department that feeds competitive information back to their insurance company management. Once the information is received, the marketing department makes suggestions for change, if they feel it makes sense. Senior management from both claims and underwriting then either agree or disagree with the recommendation(s). If consensus is reached within the insurance company departments, the product idea moves forward through the *Product Development* team, and, poof, a new product is born. The proposed product is then reviewed by other departments, such as the legal and information technology departments, prior to release.

Programming of new products is an extremely important part of the introduction of new insurance company products. In fact, this single department can cause a new product to be put on hold for a short time, or even indefinitely. Therefore, insurance companies often start the new product development process by having discussions with the information technology department to make certain that they have the capacity to provide programming support for introduction of the new product.

Since some of the items developed are "new" to a company, there may be some ambiguity concerning exactly what coverages are intended to be provided. As a result, there can be a period of time after a new product's introduction when the claims department has internal discussions concerning whether or not certain claims that have been made should or should not be paid by the insurance company.

Information Technology

The *Information Technology* department at insurance companies operates in much the same way as at other companies. They are the ones that usually "bottleneck" the entire insurance company organization. There are many more projects on the table than there are people to program requested changes. Time constraints, as well as computer system constraints also play important roles in what can be offered by insurance companies. In addition, insurance products, themselves, are much more systems-dependent than many other types of business products.

An **example** of one major project addressed by insurance companies was the "Year 2000" (Y2K) issue. It was a massive undertaking by insurance companies because it affected nearly every facet of their business - policy wording; agency contracts; suppliers and vendors, as well as simply requiring that insurance companies made certain that their future policies were issued with the correct dates.

In addition to providing programming for new products the Information Technology department is charged with maintenance of existing computer systems. This includes the updating of software programs, addressing problems that pop up at individual workstations, and solving a multitude of other technological issues as they arise.

Management

It is impossible to talk about an insurance company without mentioning its *Management*. Companies are driven by the departments previously discussed. Some companies' top-management focus on claims, some on sales, and some on underwriting. As a very *general* statement, many of the direct writer insurance company top management focus on underwriting, while companies that sell through independent agencies tend to focus on sales.

There are so many things that are beyond the control of an insurance company. Insurance is a heavily regulated industry because it deals with the "public good." Laws pertaining to insurance change frequently. **Examples** include *Proposition 103* in California several years ago – which mandated insurance price rollbacks - and more recently, the

Terrorism Risk Insurance Act – TRIA – which requires the federal government to act as a backstop in cases that involve severe damage from terrorist attacks). Indeed, legislation has a huge impact on the insurance industry. In addition, the regulatory bodies that are responsible for overseeing the insurance sector are becoming more and more liberal (pro-consumer) in their approach to dealing with conflicts that arise between insurance companies and consumers.

Other factors that have an effect on an insurance company's future include: new competitors that enter their existing marketplaces with very aggressive pricing (in this situation, carriers may need to match that pricing or risk losing market share); unexpected catastrophes that may strike up to several different times during a single year (tornadoes, hail storms, terrorism, etc.); and large losses that can deplete a company's surplus (i.e. a loss that goes "full limits" and may potentially go into an umbrella layer).

So, keeping this background in mind, I have a question. Why are a great number of insurance companies so obsessed about strategic planning 5-10+ years into the future? I have yet to figure that out. Of course it makes sense to develop action plans to address things that are currently happening, or things that might happen up to two years in the future. Included are things such as the possibility of entering additional states, business product focus and rates that will be charged for products sold.

However, my experience has been that insurance company management often spend an inordinate amount of time trying to "guess" what will happen in the general marketplace, what will happen to the overall economy, and all kinds of other things over which there is no way to accurately predict. Seldom does anyone correctly guess what the future holds for insurance.

How many people called the late-2008 ultra-bear market and the corresponding vast economic meltdown and economic recession? Did anyone foresee the terrorist attacks of September 11th that forever changed so many things in the United States? My point is that you might be lucky enough to have a good guess once or twice, but that's all it is - a guess. Yet, there exist some strategists who are so crazy that they actually believe they can determine, and plan accordingly, for the long-term impact certain future occurrences might have on the insurance industry. Please give me a break! Better yet, insurance company management should give insurance customers a break and do something more worthwhile to earn their salaries.

One example of a typical management decision that I find particularly disturbing are the decisions that are made concerning the best way to run insurance company operations. Some companies feel it is best to "centralize" operations. This means that most of the work (claims, policy issuance and underwriting) will be done out of one "centrally located" building. A year or so later, these same managers, or perhaps different managers who might currently be running the company, then decide that it would be best to "de-centralize" (have multiple operating locations) their company operations.

Another area that is constantly changing is how work is done within the confines of the insurance company. An insurance company may choose to have very linear, defined departments. An example of this is a company that has only underwriters in one department, claims adjusters in another department, marketing people in another department, etc. This same company will later decide that it would be good to have "teams" comprised of underwriters, claims personnel, and marketing representatives sitting close to each other and interacting frequently. Management might then decide to go back to their original internal structure, or some combination of the two.

Please don't get me wrong. I think that change can be good, especially at stodgy, conservative insurance companies. However, I have seen too many first-hand examples of significant change predicated upon non-logical, emotionally based decisions. For instance, a national insurance company opened a large regional office simply because the senior vice-president they had hired to lead the office wanted to be located in a specific city and state.

Round-and-round it goes, where it stops nobody in insurance senior management positions seem to know. Inordinate amounts of money are spent changing where business is done and how it is done.

In some ways, it appears that the more something costs, the less attention it attracts. For **example**, an insurance company I previously worked for changed our company name only to find out that it was so close to the way another insurance company spelled their name that we were sued to cease and desist using the new name. I wonder how many wasted dollars were spent changing back and forth. Yet, when it came to small expenses, such as spending the night at a $70 hotel, employees were required not only to document, but to obtain prior approval to justify that expense.

4

Miscellaneous Factors Affecting Insurance Companies

Reinsurance

Reinsurers "insure" the insurance company. They pay for losses that occur under the specific contract that is signed between themselves and the insurance company that they reinsure. Usually, these agreements provide reimbursement for "catastrophic" types of losses. **Examples** of catastrophes that may be reinsured include wide-spread losses that occur over a large geographical territory (such as storm damages from hurricanes and tornadoes) to the claims involving significant dollar amounts at a specific location (such as damages associated with the September 11, 2001, terrorist actions in New York).

Reinsurance protects insurance companies from paying out their entire policyholder surplus (savings) in cases where the insurance company is obligated to pay out very large dollar amounts due to payable claims submitted – usually within a very short period of time. In these situations, reinsurers reimburse companies for amounts paid out. However, it is interesting to note that reinsurance is, in some ways, nothing more than a "loan" to the insurance company. Reinsurers will recoup their payout in the form of higher prices for their reinsurance that is provided by agreement in future years.

Insurance companies typically purchase reinsurance in one of the following methods: *treaty*, *facultative* or *bordereau*. Companies can use all of these methods at the same time. **Treaty reinsurance** is negotiated across the insurance company's entire book of business according to agreed-upon criteria. For example, losses that fall within the dollar value range of $500,000 to $1,000,000. Treaties include many exclusions. One such exclusion may prohibit the insurance company from binding any business that fills propane tanks due to the potential for a large loss due to explosion.

Treaty exclusions can be overcome when the reinsurer grants an "exception" or "accommodation." Sometimes these terms are used interchangeably. Other times, "exception" refers to a "minor" allowance of something excluded by the reinsurer, while "accommodation" refers to a "major" allowance. Using my propane tank example, the reinsurer will ask several specific, detailed questions and may agree to make an accommodation based upon answers given pertaining to the specific risk characteristics. One of the most important things that a business can do if it fills propane tanks is to make certain that their refill tank is located a significant distance (i.e. 100 feet or more) from any other combustible materials – buildings, contents, vehicles, etc. If not, the reinsurer will not make an accommodation.

One ancillary benefit of working with reinsurance companies is the opportunity for insurance company underwriters to gain additional knowledge about types of risks (homeowners, auto, businesses, etc.). Reinsurance underwriters are experts in their given area and share their knowledge with the insurance company underwriters that they work with.

Facultative reinsurance is purchased on a case-by-case basis when a specific risk falls outside of values that were agreed upon within the reinsurance treaty. An example would be insuring a property exposure valued at $1,500,000. In this case, facultative reinsurance would be purchased in the amount of $500,000.

When facultative reinsurance is purchased, an additional premium must be paid to the reinsurer to pay for the additional exposure they have agreed to reinsure. Today, the purchase of facultative reinsurance is an easy process. Underwriters simply click on an icon on their computer, answer a few questions, and come up with a price for the cost of reinsurance. The reinsurance may be immediately bound and used to place the risk with the insurance company.

Bordereau reinsurance is purchased when an insurance company wishes to reinsure a specific set of risks. An example of this type of reinsurance is when a book of business is purchased from another insurance carrier and the purchasing company wishes to limit its loss exposures associated with the new book of business by purchasing reinsurance.

As reinsurance premiums to insurance companies increase, these costs are passed along to consumers in the way of policy premium increases. It is interesting to note that since the year 2000 (with the exception of the years 2001, 2002, and 2003) we have been in a "soft" underwriting cycle. A soft cycle is defined as a time when consumer insurance premiums have remained mostly flat (unchanged), or may have even decreased somewhat. Part of the cause of this phenomenon has been due to reinsurance premiums staying relatively stable, overall, as the result of reinsurance company profitability.

However, as seen in 2001, 2002 and 2003, reinsurance prices do increase from time to time, and a corresponding and a "firming" or "hardening" of the general marketplace takes place. This means that price increases will be borne by the ultimate insurance consumer.

5

Pricing

One of the basic premises behind insurance is the **Law of Large Numbers**. This holds that "as more exposure units join the statistical group, losses become more predictable." In other words, insurance companies attempt to spread the losses of a few among the many who pay insurance premiums.

Insurance companies try to write policies insuring risk exposures that will not have losses, hoping to earn an underwriting profit (an underwriting profit occurs when premiums paid into the insurance company total more than the losses paid out by the insurance company, plus expenses incurred. It does <u>not</u> include other sources of income, such as investment income).

Here's the rub. The typical insurance consumer doesn't know whether he or she is adequately covered or whether they are paying a *fair price* in the marketplace for what they have purchased. They rely almost exclusively on what their insurance agent or insurance company tells them. That can be a big mistake!

Insurance companies tell their agents not to "leave money on the table." This means they should try to sell insurance at the highest possible price while still closing the deal. In **personal lines** (auto, homeowners, etc.), there are typically pricing "tiers" that customers may qualify for. These are controlled by underwriting guidelines, for the most part, but exceptions can be made to give customers a better deal than they would normally qualify for. Equate this to paying "sticker" price for an automobile rather than obtaining a discount for the car you purchase. Most consumers have no idea that they may be able to qualify for a better price with the same company. Remember, it is in the insurance company's best interest to charge the highest possible price for their products since this helps improve their bottom line.

In **commercial lines** (businessowners, commercial property and general liability coverage, etc.), there is even more rating (pricing) flexibility. Technically, underwriters are charged with looking at characteristics of a particular business and applying "credits" or "debits" to the particular business. However, policy pricing can depend upon non-risk characteristics. One such non-risk characteristic is the market cycle. In "soft" markets, most policies have some type of credit, and much underwriting credibility is lost. In "hard" markets, the pendulum swings the other way and consumers are often charged more than their individual risk characteristics merit. This may be due to the increased price of reinsurance or due to the fact that an insurance company previously had a bad year (for example, their combined ratio – defined as the ratio of income to expenses – was over 100%).

Sometimes, pricing a new business account amounts to nothing more than an underwriter asking their agent (or the client directly) how much the client is currently paying with their incumbent company – and releasing a quote at a slightly lower price. The lower price is typically low enough that the prospective customer will want to move, but usually not as low as the company could go.

There are special tools available to underwriters when they price accounts. *Experience rating* allows certain lines of commercial business to be further discounted, depending on an individual account's past loss history.

"*A-rates*" are judgment rates applied to certain general liability codes which allow the underwriter to price this line of business however they wish (using their best judgment). For instance, if I want to insure 1,000 acres of real estate development property (land), the judgment rate could be anywhere from .01 per acre to $100 or more per acre.

"Loss costs" are additional rating factors that are used by underwriters during the premium rating process. Loss costs are typically applied to commercial business and reflect the insurance company's profitability on certain segments within a line of business. For instance, loss costs can be applied separately to commercial automobile liability, automobile comprehensive, automobile collision, and other factors which make up the total premium for commercial automobile insurance. Generally, insurance companies are able to apply additional credits through the use of loss costs. If debits are necessary, pricing may become uncompetitive.

General liability rates are usually based on sales (receipts), units, acres, or such similar measurement. General liability rates are filed with State Departments of Insurance based on "class codes," which differ according to the type of business being insured. As an example, a frozen food distributor has a class code of 13049, while a restaurant with no sales of alcoholic beverages - without dance floor - is a code 16814. Different types of businesses have different corresponding base rates.

Property rates are usually developed from Insurance Services Office (ISO) inspections. There are rate cards on file at insurance companies that shows the building construction (i.e. frame, masonry, non-combustible, etc), and fire protection (i.e. less than five road miles from the responding fire department or more than five road miles from the responding fire department). Based on the physical inspection of the property, the insurance company makes an educated guess as to the probability that this particular property will have a total loss.

The higher the probability of loss (i.e. a wooden building located fifteen miles from a responding fire department), the more premium on a "rate per $100 of value" basis the business will pay. Alternately, the better the risk from a fire protection standpoint, the lower the rate per $100 that will be charged - such as a business that has a masonry building located two blocks away from the responding fire department.

Commercial Automobiles are priced based on the type of vehicle (i.e. "heavy" - over 20,000 pounds), the radius of operation (i.e. "intermediate" - 51 to 200 miles), whether or not there is a "fleet" (5 or more units), and business usage (i.e. "service" vs. "commercial" use). In addition, underwriters look at motor vehicle records of all persons who will be driving vehicles for the business. Again, pricing tools such as experience rating, loss costs and IRPM (internal rate premium modification - in other words, the application of "credits") can be applied to reduce the "manual" rate developed. Underwriters use their judgment when applying IRPM. Some insurance companies have internal guidelines concerning when (and how much) IRPM can be applied.

However, in nearly all cases, exceptions can be given by management to bring pricing down through the application of higher credit percentages.

Many workers' compensation policies offer dividends as an incentive for a business owner to write his work comp with a particular insurance carrier. While dividends are not "guaranteed," they have a strong history of being paid on a regular basis. In addition to offering various dividend plans, some states allow companies to discount their rates through use of IRPM credits.

6

External (3rd Party) Resources

Public Adjusters

Public adjusters are claims adjusters who work directly with businesses and individuals rather than for insurance companies. Generally, public adjusters are hired in the following circumstances:

- When a significant claim occurs for which the insurance company pays less than the policyholder feels is due under the policy (policy limit issues)

- When the insurance company tells its policyholder that they will not pay for a loss which the policyholder feels should be covered (coverage issues)

- To facilitate ease of presenting a claim to the insurance company after a large and complicated loss, such as a major fire, occurs (coverage expertise and time saving issues)

Public adjusters are consumer advocates that intercede on behalf of the policyholder with their insurance company. Public adjusters are paid directly by the policyholder and must be specifically licensed in many states.

There are not a great number of public adjusters in business across the United States. As a result, it is not uncommon for these individuals to travel across the entire USA to provide services.

Insurance Consultants

Insurance consultants provide professional insurance and risk management advice and services to clients, typically on a fee-only basis. One way to look at this profession is that they *provide insurance agent performance appraisals to businesses and individuals.*

Think about it. Company employees receive annual appraisals to let them know how they are performing in their job. Good employees are patted on the back, but since no one is perfect, there are also areas of improvement that are mentioned in their performance review. Employees who are not meeting expectations may be put on a formal action plan and may ultimately be let go.

How does a business or individual know whether their insurance agent is doing a good job if a performance appraisal is never completed? Oh sure, there are plenty of "informal" and emotionally-based performance reviews that are done. But mostly, if an insurance agent remembers your birthday, takes the company CFO golfing once a year, or brings the Human Resources person responsible for insurance some kind of treat – the insurance agent's informal performance appraisal is that he or she is doing a great job!

I like the insurance company advertisement that states, "Who insures you doesn't matter. Until it does." Luckily, the vast majority of businesses and individuals never have a claim – let alone a catastrophic claim. Heaven forbid that should ever happen…but what if it does? After the claim occurs is **not** the time to find out that inadequate policy limits were in place, or that you have unwillingly been self-insuring an event that could have easily been transferred to an insurance company.

So, what specifically does an insurance and risk management consultant do? Property and casualty consultants provide exposure analysis and recommendations, assist in marketing selection and implementation, and offer other miscellaneous specialized services as the need arises. Below are some specific services provided by a typical risk management consulting firm.

Exposure Analysis and Recommendations

An insurance consultant (widely known within the insurance industry as a "risk management consultant") first conducts a detailed interview with one or more key persons in the business. Key person is generally defined as the owner or a "C" level position within an organization. This interview process provides the means to identify exposures to loss and permits the consultant to recommend appropriate actions to address the exposures identified during the interview.

Risk management consultants review an organization's insurance and risk management programs and make recommendations regarding coverage improvements and administration, as well as loss control and financing mechanisms. Specific recommendations are provided which go beyond recommending the purchase of insurance products and which focus on areas of pure risk management. Remember that insurance is just one aspect of risk management – it is a risk transfer technique.

Miscellaneous Services

Risk management consultants also provide specialized services such as:

- claims reviews and audits;

- safety program implementation and review;

- litigation support and expert witness testimony;

- evaluation of third-party administrators; captive insurance company feasibility studies;

- self-insurance analysis;

- identification of risk financing options;

- insurance claims assistance;

- broker and/or agent selection and review, and

- disaster planning implementation and review.

7

How to Get the Best Insurance "Deal"

Insurance is confusing even to those who have made it their avocation. What can an insurance buyer do to get the *best product for themselves at the most reasonable price*? Use of a good consultant or agent is paramount to wading through insurance jargon. One of the scariest things today is insurance sales over the internet or through direct mail by someone with limited insurance knowledge.

I have personally contacted companies who offer insurance products over the internet and through direct mail, and find that the representatives selling the products lack technical knowledge. Often very simple questions are confusing to them. For instance, I asked the representative to explain "automobile medical payments" coverage to me over the telephone. They failed miserably. Not only did they not explain the coverage properly, they provided incorrect information.

The main advantages of internet and direct sales methods are price and convenience. However, there are exclusive agents and independent agents who can sell at or below prices being offered over the internet or through the mail. The key is that you must find them. Certainly, the convenience of the internet and direct mail is a real factor. However, this can be countered with use of email, a fax machine or by visiting the web page of insurance agents or consultants.

How do you go about finding a good agent or consultant? The yellow pages and local newspaper advertising is a good place to start. Referrals are also a method of getting names; however, as mentioned earlier, you should not place too much weight on the fact that someone was referred to you. You should still interview the person thoroughly before allowing them to become your insurance representative.

Some questions to ask a prospective insurance agent or consultant include:

- How many years have you been a licensed agent or consultant?

- What do you consider to be your "specialty" (strongest area) and why?

- What is your weakest area? How do you deal with that area?

- What can you offer me that other agents or consultants cannot?

- Who writes your personal insurance coverage? (Many of the best agents have others write their own coverages in order to have a second set of eyes review their policies, as well as to have someone else to sue if improper coverages are written).

- How important is continuing education to you? What is the last class you took?

- What is your opinion concerning the future of the insurance industry? Give a brief description of what you feel it will look like two years from now.

- If I do business with you, who will be handling my account - you, one of your customer service representatives or someone else in your office?

- What can I expect from you in the future? How often will you review my account? What is your "renewal process?"

- What types of services can you provide besides selling insurance policies?

- Provide the names and phone numbers of ten of your most satisfied clients.

- What is the best method to communicate with you – email, telephone, fax, or other?

- Which insurance companies do you represent, and what are their "A.M. Best's" ratings?

- What are the top five insurance companies you represent based upon premium volume?

- How well does the company you are proposing to write my insurance handle claims? What is their claims reputation? Are they "slow payers" or "tough payers?"

Based upon direct feedback from clients, I can attest that Insurance Consultants play the role of "the great equalizer" in the insurance purchasing process. Fee-only consultants do not represent any insurance companies and work entirely on behalf of their clients. There is no dual fiduciary responsibility conflict since consultants have not signed contracts with any insurance companies.

Insurance consultants are free to recommend any insurance company that will do the best job for your specific needs. Some of the benefits realized by personal insurance and business insurance consumers when using a consultant include:

- specialized knowledge

- ability to obtain broader coverages

- ability to obtain lower prices

- time savings for client

- impartial 2nd opinion of current insurance program, including agent and insurance company effectiveness

8

Risk Management

As mentioned earlier, insurance is just one aspect of risk management – it is a risk transfer technique. Risk management is a broad discipline and its breadth is beyond the scope of this book. However, it is important to understand some basis risk management concepts to better understand how insurance fits within risk management parameters.

A good working definition of "risk management," attributed to Robert J. Marshburn, CRM, CIC, ARM, is "the practice of protecting an organization from financial harm by identifying, analyzing, and controlling risk at the lowest possible cost."

It is also important to understand where risk management (a risk manager) fits within a typical business organization. Refer to the "Sample Risk Management Department Organization Chart" for a snapshot view of a risk management position within a corporate organizational chart.

SAMPLE RISK MANAGEMENT DEPARTMENT
ORGANIZATION CHART

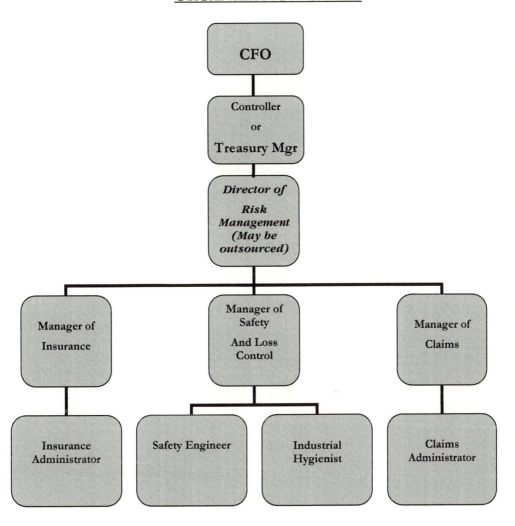

This organization chart illustrates the structure of a typical Risk Management Department at a medium-to-large-sized company. Note: the Risk Manager can perform the duties of the positions located below his/her role, or can supervise individuals who fill the stated positions.

I have also included two additional items to provide a more complete understanding of risk management. The first item is a listing of "Risk Manager Essential Responsibilities." This explains the typical duties and responsibilities of a risk manager within a general business setting.

Lastly, a risk management case study has been included in the Appendix section of this book. This case study provides some areas of consideration that a risk manager might use when analyzing a specific business situation, as well as sample answers to questions related to the case study.

It is important to keep in mind that the risk manager's **client** always makes the final decision concerning the best risk management course of action that will ultimately be taken for their specific business operations. Their decision may include some "emotional" subjective reasoning, as well as objective reasoning.

For instance, I was hired as a consultant on a project for a large, complex contracting enterprise. Part of the scope of my project was to discern whether the business should have one "master policy" with all subsidiaries named in the master policy, or whether more than one insurance policy should be written providing coverage for one or more of the subsidiary companies.

During my project, I discovered that there was a wood furniture manufacturing business that had low revenues, high losses and seemingly no redeeming qualities. Therefore, I recommended that not only should the furniture business be written on a separate policy, I also strongly suggested that the parent corporation consider selling the furniture business.

Ultimately, the decision-maker at the parent company said that he understood the reasoning for my recommendation. However, the furniture business happened to be founded by the parent company's majority stockholder's great-great grandfather and it held significant sentimental value to him. As a result, they decided to make "no change" with regards to the furniture business.

While personally disagreeing with this course of action, I fully respected my client's decision.

RISK MANAGER ESSENTIAL RESPONSIBILITIES

There is value in detailing typical responsibilities of a risk manager. Below is a list of some typical risk manager responsibilities:

- Researches, compiles and maintains insurance placement and renewal application underwriting information

- Negotiates and recommends the procurement, renewal, budgeting and record-keeping of all corporate insurance

- Analyzes coverage options, prepares and presents recommendations for placement

- Guides the establishment and implementation of loss control related operating and training procedures between business units and brokers/insurers

- Conducts site visits to identify risk exposures, maintain working knowledge of applicable codes and standards and recommend appropriate loss control solutions

- Manages the day-to-day risk management and insurance functions, ensuring that corporate policies are followed and amended as business needs change

- Identifies changes in corporate risk exposure. Coordinates issuance of insurance certificates

- Assists the Internal Audit Manager (or CEO, CFO, etc.), in the development and maintenance of risk management policies, procedures and programs necessary to mitigate identified corporate risk exposures

- Assists in the analysis and identification of risk exposures associated with contracts or agreements between the corporation and any contractor/vendor, including leases

- Provides risk transfer recommendations to mitigate company exposures

- Assists the legal department with claims management, administration and settlement

- Assists the human resource department as a loss control liaison related to safety and health, medical and worker's compensation claim areas

- Maintains and analyzes loss experience data and recommends appropriate policy changes

- Provides corporate insurance perspectives to governmental regulatory agencies, code officials and insurance companies as required

- Represents the corporation in appropriate regulatory or public safety forums

- Performs miscellaneous ad hoc analysis as required

- Develop and communicate risk management policies

- Conduct risk identification surveys to identify risk exposures

- Arranges alternative risk financing solutions (in addition to insurance), where appropriate

- Implement/monitor loss control program

- Determines cost of risk and prepares applicable allocations to cost centers

- Participate in due diligence analysis related to mergers and acquisitions

- Designs, implements and monitors claims handling and loss control procedures

- Develops and maintains a Risk Management Policy and Procedures Manual

- Develops and maintains a Risk Management Information System to identify, measure and manage risk within the organization

- Conducting alternative funding feasibility studies to identify costs and benefits of implementing transfer mechanisms beyond traditional insurance programs. Includes analysis of alternatives such as captives or self-insurance, or joining association-owned insurance companies

- Review, analysis and monitoring of overall risk management department operations, including program results and effectiveness

- Organization and administration of third-party self-insured providers

- Coordination of risk management policies with organizational mission and goals

9

The Future of Insurance

Following are some of my general thoughts concerning the future of insurance.

The trend toward more government regulation will continue. Insurance represents a large a part of a typical household's budget, remains confusing to those outside of the insurance industry, and concerns the public good. Therefore, it cannot and will not be ignored by lawmakers. McCarran-Ferguson (the law established in 1945 which gave individual states the authority to regulate their own state's insurance industry) will likely be struck down in whole or in part, and the federal government will become more active in the regulation and standardization of insurance across the United States. In fact, I initially predicted this several years ago and it has now come to fruition in the area of health insurance.

Individual states will remain active, but they will eventually take a back seat to Washington. The federal government will continue to offer some type of legislation to safeguard insurance company assets in the event of a terrorism-related catastrophe. Again, this prediction has been proven true with the passage of the Terrorism Risk Insurance Program Reauthorization Act of 2007. This 2007 law was an update of the original Terrorism Risk Insurance Act (TRIA) that was passed in 2002 as a result of the September 11, 2001, terrorist acts.

Easy-to-read policies made their first appearance many years ago. However, these should have been called "easier-to-read" policies because they are still difficult to read and understand. Companies will find ways to make their contracts easier to comprehend by people unfamiliar with insurance. More and more policies will be issued on a "businessowners package" (BOP) type of policy and fewer and fewer commercial package policies (CPP) will exist.

Alternative distribution channels will make considerable headway in future years. People will feel more and more comfortable buying over the internet and over the telephone. Insurance will continue to be viewed as a "commodity" by consumers and price will remain the number one key consideration in the average person's decision to purchase an insurance policy. Coverages and relationship with the company and/or salespersons will become a more distant second and third place, in terms of consumer importance.

The trend towards "bigger and bigger" will continue. The lines between banking and insurance and mutual funds will become further and further eroded. It will become more difficult to tell the difference between the large financial services companies because all of them will offer a broad array of financial based services.

Consumers will be able to do one-stop shopping. You will have the ability to have your checking account, savings account, money market mutual fund, car loan, mortgage, brokerage account, aggressive stock mutual fund, auto/home/business insurance all at the same institution. It will be the battle of the big companies to get all of the consumer's financial services related business.

Eventually, with this trend towards huge financial concerns there will be a backlash and resulting fallout from many customers. Often, people will be unable to get in touch with a warm body who can answer their questions at these mega-companies. Customer service, in general, will be poor and people will start viewing large insurance conglomerates much like the government - as a behemoth with lots and lots of red tape, and with whom it will be nearly impossible to get a live, knowledgeable person to address their problems. In time, people will balk at their inability to access decision-makers at these large financial institutions and there will be a trend towards smaller companies again - or at least large companies who are very decentralized and operating out of small regional offices.

Computers will certainly play a more important part in the insurance industry in the future. They will do more and more of what is currently being done by humans within the insurance company. Things such as underwriting via a set of criteria, as well as additional policy services functions, will be done by computer. Rating (pricing) of insurance and policy issuance will also become much more computerized in the future. Experimentation with automated claims payments for small-dollar claims will take place, as well. Consumers will complete their own applications for insurance direct to insurance companies – without insurance agent intervention or assistance.

The compensation model for insurance agents will continue to be at the forefront of discussions between insurance companies and their sales representatives. Insurance companies will want more work done by agents for less commission payment. Insurance agents will want to do less work for more commissions. There will ultimately be fewer and fewer "small" insurance agencies. More and more mid-size and large insurance agencies will merge to create huge insurance agency behemoths that will rival the size of some regional insurance companies.

Epilogue

I hope that this publication has provided you with valuable information about insurance companies, and that you are now able to put this knowledge to good use in protecting yourself from possible abuses that could occur in the insurance purchasing process.

Another intent of this publication is to serve as a wake-up call to the insurance industry. There are many good people doing many good things at insurance companies. And, insurance certainly <u>does</u> serve a vital purpose. Without insurance, there would be a tremendous strain on society, in general, as people would not be able to financially recover from the catastrophes that will inevitably occur. Also, people would spend such an inordinate amount of time worrying about "what might happen" in areas such as property or liability losses, that they would not be able to turn their attention to other worthwhile endeavors, including managing their busy lives and running their own businesses.

Yes, I am disappointed - and even ashamed at times - that my industry has not adequately addressed important consumer issues such as truly easy-to-read policies, making pricing understandable to the public at large, sharing information about contingency agreements, explaining in more detail why a policy might be cancelled, and offering consumers help in understanding when claims frequency might cause their insurance rates to increase.

However, it is my earnest hope that insurance companies will feel a moral obligation to address those consumer-related areas where they are weak, and that myself, and all who work in the insurance industry, will one day hold our heads even higher and become more proud in the knowledge that we are associated with one of the most important and influential industries ever created.

APPENDIX

Western Wooden Products, Inc.

Sample Risk Management
Case Study

Western Wooden Products, Inc.

Your customer is the President and CEO of Western Wooden Products, Inc. (WWP), a large privately held furniture manufacturing and repair business. They have been in business for 30 years. Sales revenues have been steadily increasing over the past five years and they now generate $150 million in annual sales and the company enjoys a healthy balance sheet.

WWP employs 250 people in the state of Wisconsin and several salespersons work for WWP who have offices in their homes which are located in states other than Wisconsin. One or more salesperson(s) is located in each of the following states: Iowa, Michigan, Ohio, Minnesota, and California.

WWP has a triple-net lease in effect. The owner of WWP formed a separate company, Products Building Leases, LLC, that owns one 100,000 square foot manufacturing building which is insured on a replacement cost basis for $25,000,000. It was built in 1970, is fully sprinklered, and is located in PC 4. There is also a storage building which contains lumber used in WWP's manufacturing process which is located five miles away from the manufacturing building.

The title to this property is also in the name of Products Building Leases, LLC. The storage building was built in 1950 and is located in PC 10. It has 50,000 square feet and is valued on an ACV basis at $1,000,000.

Business personal property is located solely at the manufacturing facility, with the exception of lumber and several pieces of machinery and equipment, such as forklifts, which are kept at the warehouse location. The total value of business personal property at the manufacturing facility is $20,000,000 (including machinery used in the manufacturing process). Lumber located at the warehouse/storage building fluctuates in value frequently, both due to the price of lumber and due to frequent inventory changes. Currently, lumber is valued at $700,000 and the equipment located at the warehouse has a schedule limit of $175,000.

WWP also owns a fleet of 100 delivery trucks, 50 of which are semi-trailer and tractor units. In addition the president of WWP owns a 2009 Mercedes Benz ML320 Bluetec SUV, valued at $50,000. It is driven mainly for personal use and is titled in the name of Western Wooden Products. The president's wife drives a 2005 Aston Martin DB9, currently valued at $75,000 and which is also titled in the name of WWP. The last private passenger auto titled in the name of WWP is driven by the president's 18 year old son that works occasionally during the summer for WWP. He has three speeding violations during the past three years and drives a 2003 Chevrolet Corvette Z06, currently valued at a mere $30,000.

WESTERN WOODEN PRODUCTS
YEAR END FINANCIAL STATEMENT

Income:

Furniture Sales	$28,000,000
Excess Lumber Sales	$ 500,000
Gross Sales:	$28,500,000

Less Cost of Goods Sold:

Lumber Costs	$14,000,000
Furniture Damaged in Mfg Process	$ 250,000
Total Costs:	$14,250,000

Gross Profit: $14,250,000

Operating Expenses:

Insurance	$ 2,500,000
Utilities (Heat and Electric)	$ 500,000
Payroll	$ 4,250,000
Rents:	
Fixed	$ 2,000,000
Total Rent	$ 2,000,000
Taxes:	$ 2,750,000
Total Expenses:	$14,000,000

Net Profit: $ 250,000

Case Analysis

1. Based on the areas we have discussed, list some of the methods you can use to identify major risk exposures to your company.

2. What are some of the techniques/tools/methods that can be used to address risk exposures?

3. Why might you want to hire a risk manager to help your organization address risk?

4. Identify contractual risk management tools/techniques that a risk manager may use when reviewing contracts.

5. What are some reasons for carrying a high deductible?

6. How would you go about allocating the cost of risk for your organization?

7. Explain the concept of Enterprise Risk Management

8. What are some of the reasons to develop a risk management policy and procedures manual?

Case Analysis

(Any type of exposure to loss based on the case study. Direct Property, Indirect Losses, General Liability, Human Resources & Employment Practices, Auto, Surety, Leases and Contracts)

Exposure	Measurement	Treatment
	Frequency Severity	
	L M S L M S	
	L M S L M S	
	L M S L M S	
	L M S L M S	
	L M S L M S	
	L M S L M S	
	L M S L M S	
	L M S L M S	
	L M S L M S	
	L M S L M S	
	L M S L M S	
	L M S L M S	
	L M S L M S	

Note: **L** = Low, **M** = Moderate, **S** = Severe

*Used with permission of the National Alliance for Insurance Education and Research

WESTERN WOODEN PRODUCTS, INC.
SAMPLE RISK MANAGEMENT ANSWERS:

1. **Based on the areas we have discussed, list some of the methods you can use to identify major risk exposures to your company.**

    1. Standardized surveys and questionnaires.

    2. Financial statements.

    3. Other records and files.

    4. Activities flow charts.

    5. Personal inspections.

    6. Discussions.

2. **What are some of the techniques/tools/methods to address the risk exposures?**

    1. Exposure avoidance.

    2. Loss prevention.

    3. Loss reduction.

    4. Segregating exposures.

    5. Contractual transfer.

    6. Retention.

3. Why might you want to hire a risk manager to help your organization address risk?

- Develop and communicate risk management policies

- Communication: internal and external

- Conduct risk identification surveys

- Arrange risk financing (including insurance placement)

- Manage litigation in conjunction with claims/legal department

- Investigate accidents

- Implement loss control program

- Contractual analysis/review leases

- Determine cost of risk

- Prepare allocations to cost centers

- Auditing of existing insurance/self-insurance programs in the property, casualty, employee benefits and pension areas

- Architect (design) of insurance programs, including both primary and excess layers

- Preparation of specifications for any and all portions of an insurance program being bid, as well as an evaluation of the responses to the specifications

- Analysis of the various funding alternatives for any particular lines of insurance to be studied

- Participate in due diligence analysis related to mergers and acquisitions

- Designing, implementing, and monitoring claims handling and loss control procedures

- Conducting feasibility studies for captives and association-owned insurance companies
- Reviewing, analyzing and monitoring overall risk management department operations, program results and effectiveness
- Coordinate risk management policies with organizational mission and goals
- Facilitate the development or purchase of a Risk Management Information System
  (RMIS)

4. Identify contractual risk management tools/techniques that a risk manager may use when reviewing contracts.

1. Hold Harmless Agreement
2. Indemnity Agreement
3. Exculpatory Clause

5. What are some reasons for carrying a high deductible?

- A credit is applied by the insurance company which lowers the price you pay for insurance.
- By carrying a high deductible you are showing the insurance company that you are willing to bear part of the risk of loss to your buildings and business personal property. This makes insurance company underwriters more comfortable with

accepting your account and may result in an overall lower price for your insurance.

- Losses incurred below your deductible threshold may be eligible for deduction on your corporate federal income taxes.

6. How would you go about allocating the cost of risk for your organization?

- Decide whether you will use an exposure-based allocation, experience-based allocation, or a combination of the two methods
- Include the following costs in your allocation system:

  1. Risk management departmental costs

  2. Outside services

  3. Retained losses (passive and active)

  4. Insurance premiums

  5. Other considerations (indirect costs)

7. Explain the concept of Enterprise Risk Management

- Enterprise Risk Management focuses on all risks that impact the company. A good working definition of Enterprise Risk

Management is "a framework for handling all of the risks facing an organization, whether insurable or not."

- Enterprise Risk Management describes an approach to risk management. It involves a wide range of tools and methodologies all designed to understand the relationship between an organization's risk profile and its impact on earnings and shareholder value.

- The four (4) main categories of enterprise risk are:
  1. Hazard/Event

  2. Financial

  3. Strategic

  4. Operational

8. What are some of the reasons to develop a risk management policy and procedures manual?

- The purpose of a policies and procedures manual is to:
  1. Reaffirm corporate policies
  2. Communicate risk management policy
  3. Communicate senior management's support for the risk management program, which includes the risk management policy, the risk management mission

statement, and the risk management policy and procedures manual

4. Define responsibility and authority

5. Familiarize personnel with exposures and procedures (risk management policy statements)

6. Provide a convenient reference - the "How To" guide

7. Convey a positive image of the risk management department

8. Detail policies and procedures in selection of third-party service providers

About the Author

Kevin L. Glaser is president of Risk & Insurance Services Consulting, LLC (RISC), a fee-only property and casualty consulting business located in Oconomowoc, Wisconsin.

Mr. Glaser began his insurance career with *American Family Mutual Insurance Group* first as a Property Adjustor, and later as a field underwriter, handling both personal lines and farm lines. Mr. Glaser then joined *Fireman's Fund* to underwrite high-value homes, umbrella policies, inland marine and automobiles of the affluent.

A management position was accepted at Tower Insurance Company, Inc., and while at Tower, the company experienced both ownership and name changes. Tower was owned by Guardian Royal Exchange, a world-wide financial services conglomerate and became known as GRE America, and later, as GRE Insurance Group. Upon purchase of another insurance company, GRE was renamed Indiana Insurance Company, and eventually became a member of the Liberty Mutual Group, a Fortune 100 company. Mr. Glaser's responsibilities have included overall results for business insurance departments and personal insurance departments, as well as rate-making and management of underwriters and support staff. In addition, Mr. Glaser was a select member of an American Reinsurance driven, company-wide consulting project whose mission was to re-engineer GRE's existing internal company structure.

Author of <u>Secret Ways to Reduce Your Worker's Compensation Costs – Things That Your Insurance Company May Never Tell You</u> and <u>Personal Lines Challenges in the Affluent Marketplace</u>, Mr. Glaser has a B.A. from Creighton University in Omaha, Nebraska, and has earned several distinguished professional insurance designations including: Chartered Property and Casualty Underwriter (CPCU); Certified Insurance Counselor (CIC); Senior Claim Law Associate (SCLA); Associate in Risk Management (ARM); Accredited Advisor in Insurance (AAI); Associate in Claims (AIC); Associate in Risk Management - Public Entities (ARM-P); and Associate in Insurance Services (AIS). Mr. Glaser has been quoted in national news publications such as **The Wall Street Journal**, **The Milwaukee Journal Sentinel**, and **The Hartford Courant** (Hartford, CT) relative to insurance issues.

Mr. Glaser is a member of **The TASA Group, Inc.** (Technical Advisory Services for Attorneys) and is recognized as a *recommended insurance expert service provider* by the A.M. Best Company. Litigation support services include the areas of commercial and personal property and casualty insurance, including: insurance policy review; coverage interpretations; assistance with pre-discovery strategies; review of denied claims to determine whether coverage might exist; detailed research; trial testimony and providing "second opinions" by reviewing key legal focus areas and identifying additional areas that may have been overlooked.

Glaser is also a Faculty Member of the nationally-recognized **National Alliance For Insurance Education & Research** (sponsor of *Society of Certified Insurance Counselors* courses), and is approved to teach sixteen hours of business insurance material, including "Commercial

Property Coverages," "Commercial Property Causes of Loss Forms," "Commercial Property Endorsements" "Commercial Inland Marine," "Case Studies," and "Businessowners Policy" courses throughout the United States. Additionally, Glaser has taught insurance-related courses for the business school of the University of Wisconsin-Whitewater, which is ranked among the top 50 business schools in the USA, and has provided long-term risk management services for the *University of Wisconsin-Milwaukee.*

Community involvement has included multiple terms as Board of Directors member and President of the *Oconomowoc Area Chamber of Commerce*, and leadership roles as President and Trustee of the local branch of a national non-profit organization. Mr. Glaser is former President of the *Nebraska Underwriters Association* and former Vice-President of the *Business Advisors Network* (business-to-business chapter). He has been an officer of the *Oconomowoc Toastmasters Club* and has been associated with the *Executive Resources Group*, a group of experienced business service providers who specialize in providing solutions to public and private sector companies.

Mr. Glaser is a national speaker in the areas of insurance and risk management, presenting to diverse groups such as *Corporate Casual*, a professional association comprised of accountants, attorneys and bankers; *The COSBE Group* (Council of Small Business Executives), the *NAPFA* (the National Association of Personal Financial Advisors); *the MRA* (Management Association); *SHERM* (Society For Human Resource Management); and *TEC* (The Executive Committee), an international group of CEOs

Mr. Glaser can be reached at Risk & Insurance Services Consulting, LLC:

158 East Wisconsin Avenue

Oconomowoc, WI 53066-3034

http://www.riscllc.com

Phone: (262) 569-0929 | Fax: (262) 569-0925 | info@riscllc.com

2516718R00066

Printed in Germany
by Amazon Distribution
GmbH, Leipzig